I Am Strong
Walking as a Warrior

Book Five

Walking with Jesus

Becoming the Best Me I Can Be

Pamela D White

All scripture quotations, unless otherwise indicated, are taken from the Holy Bible, **New King James Version©.** Copyright © 1982 by Thomas Nelson, Inc. Used by permission. All rights reserved.

Scripture quotations marked NIV are taken from the Holy Bible, **New International Version** ®, NIV ®. Copyright © 1973, 1978, 1984 by **Biblica, Inc.**® **Used by permission. All rights reserved worldwide.**

Scripture quotations marked NASB are taken from the Holy Bible, **New American Standard Bible**®, Copyright © 1960, 1971, 1977, 1995, 2020 by The Lockman Foundation. All rights reserved.

Scripture quotations marked AMP are taken from the Holy Bible, **Amplified**, copyright © 2015 by The Lockman Foundation, La Habra, CA 90631. All rights reserved. For Permission To Quote information visit http://www.lockman.org/

Scripture quotations marked ESV are taken from the ESV® Bible (The Holy Bible, **English Standard Version**®). ESV® Text Edition: 2016. Copyright © 2001 by Crossway, a publishing ministry of Good News Publishers. The ESV® text has been reproduced in cooperation with and by permission of Good News Publishers. Unauthorized reproduction of this publication is prohibited. All rights reserved.

Scripture quotations marked NLT are taken from the Holy Bible, **New Living Translation,** copyright © 1996, 2004, 2015 by Tyndale House Foundation. Used by permission of Tyndale House Publishers, Inc., Carol Stream, Illinois 60188. All rights reserved.

Scripture quotations marked MSG are taken from **THE MESSAGE**, copyright © 1993, 2002, 2018 by Eugene H. Peterson. Used by permission of NavPress. All rights reserved. Represented by Tyndale House Publishers, Inc.

Scripture quotations marked AKJV are taken from the Holy Bible, **Authorized King James Version**, The Authorized (King James) Version of the Bible ('the KJV'), the rights in which are vested in the Crown in the United Kingdom, is reproduced here by permission of the Crown's patentee, Cambridge University Press. The Cambridge KJV text, including paragraphing, is reproduced here by permission of Cambridge University Press.

Scripture quotations marked KJV are taken from the Holy Bible, **King James Version**.

A publication of Blooming Desert Ministries

ISBN 978-1-7370802-8-2 (sc print)
ISBN 978-1-7370802-9-9 (ebook)

Printed in the United States of America
Copyright © 2021 by Pamela D White
All Rights Reserved.

IngramSparks Publishing (Ingram: Lightning Source, LLC)

One Ingram Blvd., La Vergne, TN 37086

Publishing Note: Publishing style capitalizes certain pronouns in Scriptures that refer to the Father, Son, and Holy Spirit, and may differ from other publishing styles. **All emphasis in the Scriptures' quotations is the authors.** The name satan and related names are not capitalized as the author's preference not to acknowledge him, even though it violates grammatical rules.

No part of this book may be reproduced or transmitted in any form or by any means, electronic or mechanical – including photocopying, recording, or by any information storage and retrieval system – without permission in writing from the publisher. Please direct inquires to PDW Publications.

PDW PUBLICATIONS

Dedication

This book series is dedicated to you.

Everyone has opportunities to become a better version of themselves. My prayer is that this book series helps you on that journey. The Lord loves you so much He desires an intimate relationship with you. You are special to Him and He loves spending time with you. Walking and talking with Jesus every day should be the norm, not the exception. Life can bring difficult circumstances and situations. When you walk with Jesus, life events, are not only manageable but can be turned for your good.

"And we know that all things work together for good to those who love God, to those who are the called according to His purpose," Romans 8:28.

Come with me into this exploration of how you can develop a relationship with Jesus and walk with Him every day. This is an opportunity to become a better you.

Acknowledgments

The Great Commission given by our Lord and Savior Jesus Christ noted in Matthew 28:16-20 is my inspiration for this publication. Verses 19-20 state, *"Go therefore and make disciples of all the nations, baptizing them in the name of the Father and of the Son and of the Holy Spirit, teaching them to observe all things that I have commanded you; and lo, I am with you always, even to the end of the age."* This verse is the very basis for missionary work all over the globe. I have been blessed to be able to serve in a few of those missions. Missions are an amazing experience. I came to realize though that everyone cannot always do all the parts commanded in these verses. I can't always go. I didn't often get to baptize. What I realized was that I can do my part in teaching to observes the truths of the Scriptures. My desire to fulfill the teaching part of the Great Commission was the inspiration for this work. My pastor, Bishop Larry Taylor, and First Lady Desetra Taylor allowed our church to use these Bible studies in our New Life Discipleship classes for nearly twenty years. The work has also been used in prison ministries in central Illinois for as many years. The teaching has proven effective in changing many lives and discipling the children of God. Thank you, Bishop and First Lady, for teaching a balanced spiritual and natural life so I could complete this project and see the impact of the work on people's lives.

Bishop positioned me to be the director of New Life Ministries Discipleship for several years. New Life classes were designed to teach those new to Christianity or new to the church the foundational truths needed to build a solid life in Christ. During that time, this work was fine-tuned with the help and input from the dedicated, gifted, and anointed New Life teachers Minister Retta Smith, Minister James Smith, Minister Debby Henkel, Dr. Terry Husband, Minister Char-Michelle McDowell, Minister Yvonne Smith, Minister Herbert Smyer, and Professor Susan Gibson along with the encouragement and guidance of Dr. Chequita Brown and community service advocate Minister Patricia Turner. I also want to give a shout-out to Dr. Wanda Turner, nationally acclaimed minister, teacher, prophet, life coach, mentor, and best-selling author, who continued to encourage me to just publish the thing! Thanks to all of you. Each of you has made a significant impact on my life.

My dear friend and mentor, First Lady Marshell Wickware, supported the project and pushed me to publish it for years. Thanks for not giving up on me!

My life-long friend, Robin McClallen, thank you for all your support, input, and encouraging me to publish something. You have been instrumental in making me an author.

A special thanks to my husband, Brian K. White, for his patience and prayers as I spent hours and hours researching, writing, and rewriting. Thanks, BW!

Most of all thank you to the Holy Spirit and my Lord and Savior Jesus Christ. I present this work in obedience and honor to You.

Contents

Introduction	11
Understanding Spiritual Warfare	13
Exploring the Supernatural Realm	15
Preparing for Battle	19
Recognize the Enemy 18	
Recognizing the Enemy's Battle Tactics 19	
Recognize the Battlefield 22	
Attitude of a Spiritual Warrior	27
Spiritual Weapons of War	37
What's in Your Arsenal? 38	
The Blood of Jesus 38	
The Name of Jesus. 38	
Prayer and Fasting. 39	
Obedience and Submission. 39	
Praise and Thanksgiving. 40	
The Armor of God	41
Continuing the Conquest	49
Stepping Stones	53
I Am Strong	55
Glossary	57
About the Author	63

Book Five

I Am Strong
Walking as a Warrior

OBJECTIVE

This lesson prepares you for spiritual conflict. You will learn ways to stand strong when faced with spiritual adversity. This lesson outlines the spiritual weapons available to you, the Christian warrior. We will discuss ways to recognize the enemy of God and how to use the weapons of God to defeat him. In Christ, you are more than a conqueror over the enemy. It is Christ who causes you to triumph when you trust in Him.

MEMORY VERSE

"Finally, be strong in the Lord, and in the strength of His might. Put on the full armor of God, so that you may be able to stand firm against the schemes of the devil. For our struggle is not against flesh and blood, but against the rulers, against the powers, against the world forces of this darkness, against the spiritual forces of wickedness in the heavenly places. Therefore, take up the full armor of God, that you may be able to resist in the evil day, and having done everything, to stand firm." Ephesians 6:10-13 NASB.

I Am Strong

A. Understanding Spiritual Warfare
   1. Exploring the Supernatural Realm
   2. Preparing for Battle
   3. Recognize the Enemy
   4. Recognize the Enemy's Battle Tactics
   5. Recognizing the Battlefield

B. Attitude of the Spiritual Warrior

C. Spiritual Weapons of War
   1. What's in the Arsenal?
        a. The Blood of Jesus
        b. The Name of Jesus
        c. Prayer and Fasting
        d. Obedience and Submission
        e. Praise and Thanksgiving
   2. Armor of God
        a. Belt of truth
        b. Breastplate of Righteousness
        c. Boots
        d. Helmet of Salvation
        e. Shield of Faith
        f. Sword of the Spirit
        g. Stand
        h. Prayer and Supplication

D. Continuing the Conquest

Book Five

I Am Strong
Walking as a Warrior
Introduction

Spiritual warfare is a proactive approach to faith. The Lord calls His children to resist the enemy while diligently pursuing the promises of God. Living in faith is not a Sunday morning pew-warming life. It is a life active with the constant pursuit of God, no matter what attempts to stand in the way. This world is a fallen world. There are lots of difficulties and complications that occur daily. Life happens. Sometimes negative events are orchestrated by enemy forces to thwart the advance of God's kingdom. As a Kingdom Warrior, the Lord encourages routinely exercising the tactics and discipline necessary to gain spiritual strength and prepare for enemy assaults. As a Christian, you carry the promise of God with the added benefit of the Councilor, the Holy Spirit. Your Commander-in-Chief, Jesus Christ, will lead you to absolute victory. Let's see what it's like to be part of God's army.

Understanding Spiritual Warfare

Spiritual warfare is ongoing combat between the Creator and satan that began with satan's prideful rebellion. Satan's original name was Lucifer. He was an angel that was in charge of worship at the throne of God. That's a pretty impressive position. Lucifer must have thought so too. Lucifer thought of himself as greater than God. You can read about Lucifer's fall in Isaiah 14:12-14.

"How you are fallen from heaven, O Lucifer, son of the morning! How you are cut down to the ground, you who weakened the nations! For you have said in your heart: 'I will ascend into heaven, I will exalt my throne above the stars of God; I will also sit on the mount of the congregation on the farthest sides of the north; I will ascend above the heights of the clouds, I will be like the Most High'".

Did you see all of his "I will" declarations of pride? This rebellion got him thrown out of heaven along with 1/3 of the angels of heaven who followed him. All of this occurred before Satan talked to Eve in the Garden of Eden. Adam and Eve came along when God created a new creature to worship Him - people. That made Lucifer/Satan angry, and he has been trying to kill and destroy humankind ever since. As an adopted child of God and an heir in the kingdom of God, you play a part in this war by conquering satan in daily battles. Spiritual warfare exists in the unseen, supernatural realm - the raging battle between good and evil. Though the war is fought behind the scenes, the results of the attacks are very much things experienced and felt.

Exploring the Supernatural Realm

We define a realm as a domain, region, or sphere where someone or something occurs, prevails, or dominates. The spiritual realm is a highly structured and organized domain. God and His faithful angels are on one side, satan and his rebellious hierarchy of evil forces on the other. Ephesians 6:12 states, *"For we wrestle not against flesh and blood, but against principalities, against powers, against the rulers of the darkness of this world, against spiritual wickedness in high places"* KJV.

The Bible illustrates the spiritual conflict between good and evil in Genesis 3:15, *"And I will put enmity between you and the woman, and between your seed and her seed; it shall bruise your head, and you shall bruise his heel,"* AKJV. This scripture is the first mention of the Messiah and the promise of redemption along with the notification that war is imminent. The word enmity represents the conflict between satan (evil) and God (good). Everything that is God's including His people and His Son, Jesus Christ, are involved in this war.

Though spiritual warfare occurs in the unseen realm, the results can affect you right here on earth. The earthly struggles you encounter are often a reflection of the demonic opposition going on in the heavens. Daniel 10 records Daniel praying to God for help. The angels relayed the message to God and the answer sent Daniel's way. However, opposition in the heavens delayed the answer. God's angel was fighting a demon in an attempt to deliver Daniel's answer. The archangel Michael, one of God's chief princes of angels, came to assist the angel in his battle so the answer to Daniel's prayer could be delivered. The enemy doesn't want you to have your prayers answered and will do everything he can to stop your answer but you have a host of help in the unseen realm to help you do what God has for you to accomplish and to help you through the situations life brings your way. **ANGELS ARE YOUR ADVOCATES** in fighting the enemy horde. Here is the account of the angels assisting Daniel in Daniel 10:

"Then he said to me, "Do not fear, Daniel, for from the first day that you set your heart to understand, and to humble yourself before your God, your words were heard; and I have come because of your words. But the prince of the kingdom of Persia withstood me twenty-one days; and behold, Michael, one of the chief princes, came to help me, for I had been left alone there with the kings of Persia. Now I have come to make you understand what will happen to your people in the latter days, for the vision refers to many days yet to come."

When he had spoken such words to me, I turned my face toward the ground and became speechless. And suddenly, one having the likeness of the sons of men touched my lips; then I opened my mouth and spoke, saying to him who stood before me, "My lord, because of the vision my sorrows have overwhelmed me, and I have retained no strength. For how can this servant of my lord talk with you, my lord? As for me, no strength remains in me now, nor is any breath left in me."

Then again, the one having the likeness of a man touched me and strengthened me. And he said, "O man greatly beloved, fear not! Peace be to you; be strong, yes, be strong!" So when he spoke to me I was strengthened, and said, "Let my lord speak, for you have strengthened me." Then he said, "Do you know why I have come to you? And now I must return to fight with the prince of Persia; and when I have gone forth, indeed the prince of Greece will come."

Preparing for Battle

Before engaging in spiritual warfare, it's important to prepare for battle. Soldiers spend hours training for battle until it becomes a way of life and not just a job that needs to be completed. They live it and breathe it, living prepared and ready, always strategizing and honing their skills. They learn their enemy so they can use the best tactics. As a warrior in the army of God, you want to be just as prepared and trained for spiritual battles. It is important to know your enemy. The best way to do that is to meditate on the Word of God and develop your relationship with the Lord. When financial institutions train people to recognize counterfeit money, they do not give them the counterfeit to study. Their training includes handling the real thing. They become so familiar with authentic bills that when counterfeit is handed to them; it is easily recognized. This is how the Lord wants you to prepare for battle with the enemy. You are to become so familiar with the ways and will of the Lord that when the counterfeit makes an appearance; you recognize it immediately and handle it accordingly.

Recognize the Enemy

Remember that satan is an ancient enemy. He existed long before God created man and placed him in the Garden of Eden. The first time he is seen in the Bible is when he is deceiving Eve and tempting Adam. Satan is treacherous and cunning. He has had a lot of practice lying and deceiving people. John 8:44 describes Satan's character,

"He was a murderer from the beginning, and does not stand in the truth, because there is no truth in him. When he speaks a lie, he speaks from his own resources, for he is a liar and the father of it."

EVERYTHING SATAN WHISPERS TO YOU IS A LIE. He doesn't even know how to speak the truth. Even if it sounds true, it isn't. That's his specialty—making lies seem like truth—deception. He is very good at it. However, Genesis 3 seals his fate. The Bible barely got started when satan botched it again and messed with Adam. That's when the Lord told satan it was over for him and his ultimate demise would come from the very seed of the woman he had deceived. Messiah would come as a Man who would destroy satan forever. That doesn't mean the enemy has stopped trying to defeat humankind. He hates you, first because you are a treasured creation and second because you have the breath of God in you. When you accept Jesus as your Savior, you gave the enemy another reason to hate you because now you are an heir to the Kingdom and have an uncanny ability to praise and worship. Remember that worship was Lucifer's position in heaven. You now have his position as a worshiper and he does not like that at all. Satan is a powerful being. However, his tactics are weak against the powerful weapons of wisdom and holiness. The Lord has equipped you to defeat the enemy. Matthew 10:16 states, *"Behold, I send you out as sheep in the midst of wolves. Therefore be wise as serpents and harmless as doves"*. Wisdom is one of your greatest weapons. With wisdom, you win battles before you ever fight them. Therefore, every battle should begin on your knees in prayer. God will give you the tactics and wisdom needed to be the victor.

RECOGNIZING THE ENEMY'S BATTLE TACTICS

To better prepare to fight the enemy of your soul, it is important to understand how the enemy attacks. When you realize the enemy's tactics and how they contrast with the goodness of God, you are well on your way to victory.

You are a three-part being. You are a spirit that has a soul and lives in a body. The enemy can attack each of these parts.

- **BODY**—The anatomy and structure of the body are traditionally classified with five senses: sight, smell, hearing, taste, and touch. The body is also the house for the spirit and soul of man. Satan attempts to inhibit the will of God by attacking the physical body, both internally and externally with sickness, disease, and injury.

- **SOUL**—The anatomy of the soul includes the heart, mind, will, and emotions. You can access the soul through imagination, consciousness, memory, and reason. One of the enemy's most favorite tactics is manipulation through confusing the mind.

Lies and deceptions create confusion. The enemy is the father of lies. He is very good at making lies seem like perfect truth and will groom an individual to believe the most bizarre lies to distract them from God's purpose and destiny while creating doubt in the mind.

- **SPIRIT**—Your spirit is your God-consciousness. It is the part of you that connects to God, understands the scriptures, and has the wisdom and knowledge of how to apply God's truth. Your spirit is the part of you can discern or recognize the difference between truth and lies. The spirit receives impressions from the body and soul and then interprets them through the tools of the spirit, which are faith, hope, love, prayer, and worship. Therefore, it is so important to feed your spirit with the Word of God and worship. **A WELL-FED SPIRIT CAN DISCERN TRUTH** a lot more easily than a malnourished spirit. A starving person will eat just about anything, things that if they were not starving, they wouldn't even consider eating. The well-nourished person is much more selective and discerning of the food they ingest. Such is the state of your spirit. Well-fed spirits won't eat just anything. The enemy wants to destroy your faith, hope, love, prayer life, and your worship of God. His purpose in attacking your spirit is to extinguish your fellowship with God.

"Beloved, do not believe every spirit, but test the spirits, whether they are of God; because many false prophets have gone out into the world," 1 John 4:1.

THE ENEMY'S BATTLE TACTICS

The elements	Organs, cells	Heart, mind, will, emotions	God-Consciousness
What it consists of	5 senses—sight, hearing, touch, smell, taste	Imagination, consciousness, memory, reason	Faith, hope, love, joy, prayer, worship
What it does	Serves as a house for the soul and spirit	Creates impressions from the senses and surroundings	Interprets impressions from the soul and body
How it's attacked	Attack is physical both external & internal—sickness, disease, injury	Attack is through manipulation, confusion, lies, deceptions	Attack causes hopelessness, doubt, isolation
Purpose of the enemy attack	satanic attack will inhibit the will of God	Creates doubt in the believer's mind	Tries to destroy fellowship with God

RECOGNIZE THE BATTLEFIELD

Every war has great battlefields recorded in history books. WWI had the Battle of Marne and Verdun. WWII had the Battle of the Bulge, Pearl Harbor, and Normandy. Your greatest battlefield is your mind. The enemy can't read your mind, but he studies you and learns your responses to different situations. With this information, he will attempt to manipulate your thoughts and decisions through pride, anxiety, doubt, paranoia, depression, lies, and his favorite tool - fear. Your thoughts and feelings determine your will and purpose. So the enemy is adamant in distracting you. He does not want for one minute for your will to line up with God's will, and he certainly doesn't want you to fulfill your purpose.

Another battlefield is your bodily senses. The enemy will tempt you with desires and cravings. He will try to make your body sick and unhealthy. One of his favorite attacks is to cause addictions. As a human, you are born with sin-nature because of the fall of Adam. Sin nature makes your body want to give in to the temptations and cravings the enemy uses to distract and entangle you. Sometimes Christian lingo calls this flesh or carnal nature. Paul bumped into carnal or fleshly nature with the Corinthians. In 1 Corinthians 3:3 Paul asks the Corinthian church a couple of questions regarding their conduct. *"You are still carnal. For where there are envy, strife, and divisions among you, are you not carnal and behaving like mere men?"* Carnal-mindedness puts you at war against God instead of fighting with God on His team. Romans 8:7 states, *"Because the carnal mind is enmity against God; for it is not subject to the law of God, nor indeed can be."* The enemy is after generations. He will work on entrapping one generation so they pass their iniquity to the next generation where he builds on that iniquity which multiplies the problem for the next generation and so it goes for generations. The good news is that **GOD GIVES YOU WEAPONS** to overcome the temptations of your flesh and the distractions of your mind. We are going to go into some detail about the weapons God has provided to equip you. They are not weapons like we know in the world systems but spiritual weapons, perfect for battling a spiritual enemy. 2 Corinthians 10:4-6 states,

"For the weapons of our warfare are not carnal but mighty in God for pulling down strongholds, casting down arguments and every high thing that

exalts itself against the knowledge of God, bringing every thought into captivity to the obedience of Christ, and being ready to punish all disobedience when your obedience is fulfilled."

Not only do you have to battle your thoughts and your flesh or carnal nature, but you battle against world systems. Their division of labor, which affects economic growth and decline, defines the various socioeconomic systems around the world. The enemy wants to control that economy which directly affects your income. When he controls your income, he has power over you. His wants to keep you in poverty, want, need, insufficiencies and stress if he can. If you have wealth, his tactic is to trap you into serving your money and develop greed for more money and more power. Despite the many avenues the enemy uses to get to you, God has provided for you. 1 Corinthians 10:13 reminds,

"No temptation has overtaken you except such as is common to man; but God is faithful, who will not allow you to be tempted beyond what you are able, but with the temptation will also make the way of escape, that you may be able to bear it."

Whatever tactic Satan is using, his primary objective is to render you spiritually ineffective and make it even worse for your children and your children's children. He will do everything he can to distract the mind, tempt the body and confuse the soul. Therefore, he searches the areas of your life until he finds where you are most vulnerable, then he will begin a systematic assault. John 10:10 exposes the enemy's agenda and Jesus' solution to his assault on you. *"The thief comes not, but for to steal, and to kill, and to destroy: I am come that they might have life, and that they might have it more abundantly"* AKJV.

Some Common Tactics satan uses to Deceive, Confuse, and Manipulate

Depression	Pornography	Nicotine	Adultery
Anxiety	Masturbation	Witchcraft	Pride
Paranoia	Homosexuality	Sickness	Disobedience
Suicide	Disease	Drugs	False Religion
Lying	Alcohol	Fornication	Fear

Attitude of a Spiritual Warrior

Bible teacher and author Charles Swindoll said, "The remarkable thing is we have a choice every day regarding the attitude we will embrace for that day. We cannot change our past... we cannot change the fact that people will act in a certain way. We cannot change the inevitable. The only thing we can do is play on the one string we have, and that is our attitude. I am convinced that life is 10% what happens to me and 90% of how I react to it. And so it is with you... we are in charge of our Attitudes." **(Swindoll, 2020)**

You can decide on your reaction before an event even occurs. You can choose to be a winner and victor, no matter what life throws at you. Perspective is very important. It's important to understand that you are in a war, you are a well-equipped warrior, and God is your protector. Godly standards are the basis for a victorious attitude. A victorious mindset begins by understanding who you are and who your God is. *Romans 12:2 "And be not conformed to this world: but be you transformed by the renewing of your mind, that you may prove what is that good, and acceptable, and perfect, will of God" AKJV.* Let's look at some mindsets that need to be renewed and ways to keep a victorious warrior's attitude.

- **Attitude of Prayer**. The first place to prepare for battle is on your knees. Prayer begins with faith. After all, if you don't believe there is a God who is listening and communicating, what's the point? So first you must believe and know He hears your prayers. A warrior's prayer should be **PERSISTENT**. Jesus admonished in Luke 18:1b, *"That men always ought to pray and not lose heart"*. Prayer only works when it lines up with God's will. Jesus instructed in Matthew 6:10 for prayer to include, *"Your kingdom come. Your will be done on earth as it is in heaven"*. One aspect of prayer often overlooked is the power of thanksgiving. Thanking God shows Him you believe He is working in your life, are grateful for what He's done and what He's doing. Prayer develops your relationship with the Lord, which keeps your spiritual attitude centered. For more on prayer, please see "No Secrets."

- **Attitude of Balance**. It is important to keep a balanced Biblical view to be an effective spiritual warrior. You need balance physically, psychologically, relationally, and spiritually. Physical involves work, play, and exercise. Psychological aspects include emotional and mental health. Relational includes family, friends, and co-workers. Spiritual balance involves trusting and obeying God. Extremism in any of these areas will lead to an unbalanced life which will open doors, allowing the enemy to wreak havoc in your life. There is an old saying that, "You can fall off the log on either end." You can be too radical in any of these areas or too lazy. Too conservative or too liberal. Too much exercise or too many donuts. Too much work or too much play. Too much stress or too much indifference. Spiritual extremes can lead you into false doctrine and division or lethargy, which increases that old carnal, selfish mind. Maintaining balance in your life provides a sure footing for winning battles. 3 John 2 says, *"Beloved, I pray that you may prosper in all things and be in health, just as your soul prospers."* The Lord's heart wants every part of your life is healthy. Then the enemy's opportunities to destroy you are greatly reduced and you have more opportunities to live prosperously.

- **Attitude of Reality.** Some religions ignore that there is an enemy and others that deny there is an enemy at all. The enemy is real. Satan exists and has an army of angels to help him in his rebellion. He has intellectual ability and a gamut of emotions. He has an arsenal of temptations Ephesians 6:11 calls 'wiles.' *"Put on the whole armor of God, that you may be able to stand against the wiles of the devil."* Some people think the enemy is bold and raucous. He can be, but often he is very subtle and sneaky. Satan even knows the Scriptures. Remember, his first job was the worship leader at the throne of God. He will attempt to twist scripture just enough to trap you in deception and those deceptions can entrap you. There was a woman who lived her life in bondage because of the scripture she quoted as, "I will never leave you nor forsake you as long as you do my will." That is not what the scripture says, but that is what she was tricked into believing, so her entire life had been in bondage to doing works to earn God's presence in her life and when she failed, she felt the Lord had left her. When she learned the truth of what that scripture said, that the Lord never leaves or forsakes you, ever, she was freed from the bondage. See how subtle and tricky the enemy can be? He can even appear as a good thing to snare you. The enemy will do everything in his power to prevent you from accepting the salvation of God and to hinder or stop your spiritual growth. He attempts to infiltrate everything God has instituted in His Word, such as the church, marriage, and government. He hates anyone who professes Jesus as Lord, anyone who is a descendant of Israel, any church that is serving God, and most of all Jesus Christ. Though the enemy is real and determined to stop God and His people, his only promise is a promise of failure. God has equipped you with everything it takes to defeat the enemy. You just have to use the weapons provided to you. No worries, be happy. Hakuna matata.

- **Attitude of Victory.** God provided for your victory. God let satan know in Genesis 3 that he was fighting a losing battle. Throughout time, the Lord has reminded satan that his ultimate demise is imminent. God laid out the plan of destruction in much detail in the book of Revelation as the final climactic reality of finality. The Lord also repeatedly tells His people that they are victors. **VICTORY IS YOURS**. You are guaranteed success when you follow God. Follow the Word of God and victory is yours. If you try to fight on your own without Jesus, Holy Spirit, or the Word, your victory is not solid. 2 Corinthians 2:14 states *"Now thanks be to God, which always causes us to triumph in Christ, and makes manifest the aroma of his knowledge by us in every place"* AKJV. Those two little words are often overlooked, 'in Christ.' Triumph comes 'in Christ.' Without Christ, you can get whooped pillar to post every turn you make. When Jesus died and conquered death by raising Himself from the dead, He defeated satan and his demonic army with one fell swoop. Colossians 2:15 declares, *"Having disarmed principalities and powers, He made a public spectacle of them, triumphing over them in it"*. Jesus didn't just beat the enemy. He made a big deal about it. Knowing you already won will change the way you approach life. You can walk into situations with the powerful knowledge that Christ already won and you are a victor in Him.

Ok, I heard you. It doesn't always feel like victory, does it? If Christ already won, then why are you still fighting? Great question. Remember, you're your history lessons. When World War II was over, there were some areas in the South Pacific where the enemy had not heard or refused to acknowledge the war was over. They continued to fight, take prisoners of war, torture, and cause havoc for a long time. The treaty was signed and the fighting had ceased except in these reclusive pockets. Enemy soldiers still conducted battle, although the war was over and they had lost. Peacemaking forces had to go into these areas and rescue prisoners, stopping the enemy forces from continuing their attacks. You are the peacemaking force sent into an enemy camp. As the warrior of God, He sent you to stop the enemy from continuing his attack, taking back the prisoners of war. You were sent to remind the enemy he has lost and you are on the victorious team. So do not despair when the battle is tough. Know that the war is over, the treaty is signed, and you are sent to evict the enemy. Then put up a victory flag and celebrate!

- **Attitude of Dominion.** God builds dominion into man's DNA. When God created all things, He gave dominion or rule to man. God gave Adam dominion in Genesis 1:26 and repeated in 1:28 Adam's dominion over the fish of the sea, the fowl of the air, over the animals on the earth and everything that creeps on the earth. Throughout the Old Testament, the Word reminds the Israelites of their dominion, even though they sometimes failed to recognize their position as God's chosen people. Colossians 1:16 tells us *"For by him were all things created, that are in heaven, and that are in earth, visible and invisible, whether they be thrones, or dominions, or principalities, or powers: all things were created by him, and for him"* AKJV. God created everything, and everything is under his power. So it is completely up to Him who has that power and He has chosen you. When Jesus arrives on earth as a man in the New Testament and completes the work of redemption through His death and resurrection, a new level of dominion comes into play. Paul tells the church in the *Ephesians 1:15-23,*

"Therefore I also, after I heard of your faith in the Lord Jesus and your love for all the saints, do not cease to give thanks for you, making mention of you in my prayers: that the God of our Lord Jesus Christ, the Father of glory, may give to you the spirit of wisdom and revelation in the knowledge of Him, the eyes of your understanding being enlightened; that you may know what is the hope of His calling, what are the riches of the glory of His inheritance in the saints, and what is the exceeding greatness of His power toward us who believe, according to the working of His mighty power which He worked in Christ when He raised Him from the dead and seated Him at His right hand in the heavenly places, far above all principality and power and might and dominion, and every name that is named, not only in this age but also in that which is to come. And He put all things under His feet, and gave Him to be head over all things to the church, which is His body, the fullness of Him who fills all in all."

Isn't that amazing? Through Christ, you have dominion and access to the greatness of power over every principality, power, might, and dominion (God covered all levels of the demonic hierarchy). Paul stated you need wisdom and revelation to get that concept. The ironic thing is the enemy knew about your dominion long before you knew it yourself. He knew it before you were even born. That's why he has worked so hard in trying to stop you from understanding who you are and the power you have over him. Once you recognize the dominion and power available to you, the attacks of the enemy are like mosquito bites. They are no longer consequential. Dominion is not so you can have power over other people. You are always to have a heart willing to serve your fellow man. Dominion over God's creatures and creation should always be with the spirit of stewardship and the understanding that the earth is the Lord's and not ours. The dominion Paul is describing is over your spiritual enemy, the devil, and his cohorts.

- **Attitude of Obedience**. As a Christian, you are called to be obedient to God in the big things and the little things of everyday life. That doesn't mean that as a Christian you are subject to a set of rules. This is a misnomer the enemy uses to keep people away from Christianity. Obedience means you are in submission to the things that God requires of you to do and the things He asks you to do. There are two main and important things God asks of you. Matthew 22 37-39 explains those two commandments. *"Jesus said to him, "'You shall love the LORD your God with all your heart, with all your soul, and with all your mind.' This is the first and great commandment. And the second is like it: 'You shall love your neighbor as yourself.'"* There you have it. **LOVE GOD. LOVE PEOPLE.** Pretty simple. Often it feels complicated and intricate. Excuses are made and reasoning tells why either of these commands cannot be accomplished. But it really is just that simple. Strip away the excuses, discard the reasoning, accept the truth and just love somebody and love your God. The enemy doesn't want you to do either of these things. So, he throws all kinds of roadblocks into your path of life. Then when God asks you to do something, because of the roadblocks, it seems impossible to you or makes a simple daily request seem irrelevant or an imposition. The Lord may ask you to do something as simple as opening a door for someone. The enemy will try to get you so wrapped up in yourself and your problems that you miss these simple destiny opportunities to bless someone. Sometimes things might seem bigger than what you can do. I have news for you. They just might be too big for you! That's the good news. The great news is that God equips you for every task He asks you to do either by enhancing your abilities or He will do it through you if you allow Him that freedom. That's called the anointing. The enemy of your soul does not want you to have a heart of obedience. He prefers a heart of rebellion because it reflects his attitude. 2 Corinthians 13:5 says to *"Examine yourselves as to whether you are in the faith. Test yourselves."* Throughout the scriptures, warnings appear to watch yourself, guard yourself, and give heed to yourself. You are your own master to watch and make sure you are keeping an attitude of obedience by loving God and others.

- **Attitude of Focus.** Distractions, distractions, distractions. Everybody needs something from you, time limits your abilities, stress weighs you down, and sleep is restless. **DISTRACTIONS** come through complications, confusion, disturbances, amusements, entertainment, agitations, preoccupations, interferences, health issues, mental stressors, and a whole slew of other directions. It is the ADHD of the spirit; the enemy of focus. The Word guides you to focus on some specific things. The first priority is to focus on God. When Moses focused on God, his face became radiant. Psalm 34:5 says that *"They looked to Him and were radiant, and their faces were not ashamed."* When you focus on God, He radiates through your life. You are also to focus on your eternal life. When you remember that your life is not just for today, but that this life is a stepping-stone to your eternal life. 2 Peter 3:13 describes this focus, *"Nevertheless we, according to His promise, look for new heavens and a new earth in which righteousness dwells."* The Word reminds you to focus on things above. *Colossians 3:2 "Set your mind on things above, not on things on the earth."* Remember, you are not alone. God is with you and helping you in prayer and decisions. Therefore, it is necessary to focus on the path God has prepared for you, a path of godliness and righteousness. *Proverbs 9:6 "Forsake foolishness and live, and go in the way of understanding."* Psalms 119:112 instructs you to focus on the Lord's decrees or instructions, *"I have inclined my heart to perform Your statutes forever, to the very end."* As mentioned before, the Lord may instruct you to do some things you don't know how to do. Physicians told me I had a brain tumor. That diagnosis is not an easy one to hear. I could not get through that process on my own, but focusing on God's word, receiving His grace and healing brought me through successfully healed and victorious. 1 Peter 1:13 expresses the need to focus on God's grace for help through every situation, *"Therefore gird up the loins of your mind, be sober, and rest your hope fully upon the grace that is to be brought to you at the revelation of Jesus Christ."* You may see a common theme through these avenues of focus. They all lead to special lensed spiritual eyeglasses that reveal the most important focus, Jesus Christ. Focusing on Jesus makes it possible to endure the trials and storms of life. Hebrews 12:2 tells you to *"looking unto Jesus, the author and finisher of our faith, who for the joy that was set before Him endured the cross, despising the shame, and has sat down at the right hand of the throne of God."* Distractions are everywhere. Maintaining focus will help you recognize distractions for what they are, the cockleburs of life, and push them aside or sidestep them so you can continue your walk. For those of you who did not grow up in the Midwest where cockleburs grow in abundance, a cocklebur is a weed that develops these small pods with fishhook-like spines that grab onto your clothing. After running through a patch of cockleburs, you find them stuck to your pants, socks, and shoelaces. They are an annoyance and can be quite painful when you dislodge them. They are a painful distraction from a happy race. Paul sums it up nicely in Philippians 4:8 *"Finally, brothers, whatever things are true, whatever things are honest, whatever things are just, whatever things are pure, whatever things are lovely, whatever things are of good report; if there be any virtue, and if there be any praise, think on these thing."* AKJV.

Spiritual Weapons of War

The idea of engaging in a spiritual war may seem scary. However, you have no reason to fear. God has not left you defenseless. He equipped you with the tools needed to fight this enemy. Not only has God provided multiple weapons, but He has already given you victory. 2 Corinthians 10:4 confirms the power of your weapons. *"For the weapons of our warfare are not carnal, but mighty through God to the pulling down of strong holds"* KJV. The list of weapons is extensive and powerful. Here are some major weapons God has placed in your arsenal. There have been entire books written about each of these subjects. I encourage you to do some reading on your weapons to better understand how to use them. Here we are just going to give a synopsis.

What's in Your Arsenal?

These are weapons available to you, but that also requires something from you such as an action or speech. Soldiers don't just own swords. They know how to use them and when to use them. These are weapons available for you to use as you battle the enemy of God.

- **The Blood of Jesus.** Just like the old hymn declares, there is power in the blood of Jesus. The blood of Christ is a precious gift that redeems the sinner and restores fellowship with the Father. Colossians 1:13-14 *"He has delivered us from the power of darkness and conveyed us into the kingdom of the Son of His love, in whom we have redemption through His blood, the forgiveness of sins"*. The **BLOOD OF JESUS** brings peace with God. The blood cleanses from sin and the blood gives you power over the devil. Revelation 12:11 *"And they overcame him by the blood of the Lamb and by the word of their testimony, and they did not love their lives to the death."* Jesus defeated the enemy with the ultimate sacrifice and the shedding of His blood. Satan fears the blood of Christ. Declare the blood of Christ over your life, situations, and loved ones. The blood of Christ protects, delivers, brings forgiveness and peace.

- **The Name of Jesus.** His name is exalted above all principalities, powers, and every name that is named. Jesus is the name above all names, which means His power is greater than any man, beast, angel, or demon. Philippians 2:9-11 *"Therefore God also has highly exalted Him and given Him the name which is above every name, that at the name of Jesus every knee should bow, of those in heaven and those on earth and of those under the earth, and that every tongue confess that Jesus Christ is Lord, to the glory of God the Father"*. Speaking the name of Jesus requires the enemy to bow to the majesty of the King. Sometimes, all I can say is, "Jesus, Jesus, Jesus, Jesus, Jesus." And that was enough to conquer the situation.

- **Prayer and Fasting.** Matthew 17:14-21 tells the story of a boy who had a demon. The disciples had tried to deliver the boy from the power of the demon, but they had failed. The boy's father pleaded with Jesus to help the boy since the disciples could not figure out how to free the child from the demon. Jesus rebuked the demon which immediately released the boy. The disciples later asked Jesus why they could not perform this feat. *"So Jesus said to them, "nothing will be impossible for you. However, this kind does not go out except by prayer and fasting".* Prayer and fasting take discipline and planning. They show your humility and willingness toward the things of God. Through prayer and fasting, you will gain victory over demons and demonic assaults.

- **Obedience and Submission.** Obedience is agreement with God's Word. Submission is yielding to that Word in meekness. Obedience and submission work together to defeat the enemy. This powerful tool makes the devil run. Walking in obedience to God requires a decision on your part to trust the Word of God. Submission requires a choice to let God be in charge. James 4:7 *"Submit yourselves therefore to God. Resist the devil, and he will flee from you,"* KJV. There is absolutely nothing the enemy can do when you are walking in obedience and submission. He turns tail and runs.

- **Praise and Thanksgiving.** When you exalt and worship God, Satan leaves. Philippians 4:4; 6-70 *"Rejoice in the Lord always: and again I say, Rejoice... Be careful for nothing; but in every thing by prayer and supplication with thanksgiving let your requests be made known to God. And the peace of God, which passes all understanding, shall keep your hearts and minds through Christ Jesus,"* AKJV. Exalting God through praise and thanksgiving reminds the enemy who's in charge. The purpose of praise and worship is to glorify God. That the enemy hates it is just a perk. It isn't always easy to offer praise and thanksgiving. Sometimes, it takes some forethought to figure out something in which to give thanks. When depression and despair try to overtake you, when the world is pressing on every side, you may wonder if God has even noticed you. In his letter to the Corinthians, Paul acknowledges their struggle and his own. 2 Corinthians 4:8-9 *"We are hard-pressed on every side, yet not crushed; we are perplexed, but not in despair; persecuted, but not forsaken; struck down, but not destroyed."* Paul reminds his readers that you have been given life, grace, deliverance, and carry the glory of God within your earthen body, therefore *"cause thanksgiving to abound to the glory of God* (v.15)."

The Armor of God

Now that you know what is in your arsenal, let's talk about what you should wear to the battle. The Armor of God is the **COMBAT EQUIPMENT** of a Christian warrior who fights against spiritual wickedness. Paul used the battle armor of the Roman soldier to help Christians understand the protection they have in Christ. Satan is cunning and deceitful. His strength exceeds your natural abilities. Therefore, you must *"put on the whole armor of God"* to overcome his attacks. The Armor of God has both offensive and defensive designs. The armor equips you to engage the enemy and destroy his plan while protecting you from harm during spiritual battle. Ephesians 6 goes into great detail describing your battle clothes.

Ephesians 6:10-18 *"Finally, my brethren, be strong in the Lord and in the power of His might. Put on the whole armor of God, that you may be able to stand against the wiles of the devil. For we do not wrestle against flesh and blood, but against principalities, against powers, against the rulers of the darkness of this age, against spiritual hosts of wickedness in the heavenly places. Therefore take up the whole armor of God, that you may be able to withstand in the evil day, and having done all, to stand. Stand therefore, having girded your waist with truth, having put on the breastplate of righteousness, and having shod your feet with the preparation of the gospel of peace; above all, taking the shield of faith with which you will be able to quench all the fiery darts of the wicked one. And take the helmet of salvation, and the sword of the Spirit, which is the word of God; praying always with all prayer and supplication in the Spirit, being watchful to this end with all perseverance and supplication for all the saints."*

Now let's look at each of these items of your armor to get a better picture of what each means for you today.

- **Belt of Truth.** In the natural, the belt is the central piece of weaponry that holds all the other pieces of the body armor in place. Without this piece, the rest of the armor is not secure. The pieces are loose and disjointed, allowing gaps in the armor. Since this piece is so vital, you must understand the 'truth' this is referring to. The Truth is the Word of God. God's Word is the only unchangeable, reliable Truth. This truth closes gaps in your armor and makes the rest of your defense secure. Truth thwarts the lies and deceptions of the enemy. When you wear the belt of truth, not only does it hold your spiritual armor in place, it strengthens you against the lies and deception of Satan.

- **Breastplate of Righteousness.** The breastplate protects the heart and other vital organs against attacks. When engaging in a spiritual battle, you must choose righteous living, which guards your heart with holiness, righteousness, and purity. Proverbs 4:23 reminds us, *"Above all else, guard your heart, for everything you do flows from it."* Every decision, every action, every thought originates from your heart. Therefore, it is important to guard the heart against the attack of the enemy. You guard your heart by making decisions according to righteousness. *"Righteousness guards the person of integrity,"*

Proverbs 13:6a NIV. You will come across many crossroads in your life. These are those 'what would Jesus do' moments. Righteous decisions at these crucial moments g0uard and protect your heart from the mess the enemy is trying to create around you.

- **Boots/shoes.** During Bible times, the Romans wore heavy leather shoes when dressed for battle. There were hobnails on the tips and the back of the heel. The bottom of the boot was heavily spiked for stability in hand-to-hand combat. There were also special pieces that protected the lower legs, much like soccer shin guards, but much stronger and larger to protect the legs from breaking. Paul is referring to these army boots when he says your feet are shod with the gospel of peace. These shoes speak of the firm foundation you have in Christ when you believe the Gospel. The Gospel is the 'good news' or account of Jesus' life. The enemy can attempt to knock you over, break your legs, shove you down and kick you silly, but you have stability and strength through the Gospel truth. God's peace protects you and you can stand strong while the turmoil of life rages around you.

- **Helmet of Salvation.** The helmet protected the soldier from the deadly blows of the enemy directed at the head. As discussed previously, your thought realm is a major battleground. The enemy is relentless in telling you how worthless, incapable, incompetent, powerless, and useless you are. Maybe you are that person who doesn't feel powerless. Maybe your deception is to feel like whatever comes your way you can handle on your own and you don't need God. Either thought pattern is dangerous and deadly. The enemy bombards you with thoughts that are not your own and attempts to distract and confuse you with lies. The truth of salvation is your protection from all these lies. In Christ, you have purpose and destiny. The Lord equipped you to accomplish great things. The Lord loves you because you are important to Him. Paul declares in 1 Corinthians 2:16 that you *"have the mind of Christ."* Wearing salvation as your helmet protects your mind from fatal attacks as lies and confusion. When you believe in who you are in Christ, your helmet is doing its work of protection.

- **Shield of Faith**. One shield used by Roman soldiers was tall and covered with leather. They also carried a small shield used in close-contact warfare. The soldier would keep the leather oiled so it would remain flexible and deflect enemy arrows. Before a battle, the soldiers would soak their shields in water as a defense against fiery darts or arrows in fierce attacks. Your shield is your faith. Faith is complete trust and confidence that God is who He says He is, Jesus was God in the flesh who died and resurrected to free you from sin, and that what God has said will happen really will happen because His Word is true. When you carry your faith as a shield, then doubt, unbelief, and confusion, those fiery darts of the enemy, cannot penetrate your belief system. When you invite the Holy Spirit to saturate your confidence with the oil and water that soaks your faith, then your shield of faith quenches all the fiery darts the enemy fires at you.

- **Sword of the Spirit**. The sword is a weapon intended for hand-to-hand combat. There are different swords for face-to-face encounters with the adversary. Your spiritual sword is the **WORD OF GOD**. Hebrews 4:12 declares *"For the word of God is living and powerful, and sharper than any two-edged sword, piercing even* *to the division of soul and spirit, and of joints and marrow, and is a discerner of the thoughts and intents of the heart."* When in face-to-face conflict with the enemy, speaking the Word of Truth delivers deadly blows on the enemy. Jesus encountered Satan after He had fasted for forty days in the wilderness. Satan came to Jesus with three grand temptations, lies, and twisted scriptures. Jesus thrust back at this sly attempt to move Him from His purpose with quick jabs of the Word of God and the enemy left Him. You have this same weaponry in the Word. When the enemy whispers you are weak, you speak Joel 3:10 and tell him, *"I am strong."* When the enemy declares you are sick or diseased, you declare 1 Peter 2:24 *"by His stripes, you were healed."* The Word has the answer for every attack the enemy will bring. Your sword thrust is faithfully speaking the Word of Truth.

- **Stand**. Ephesians 6 says that after you have done everything you know to do, stand. You fought the battle and hung onto faith. You spoke the Word and made the right choices, yet things still seem bleak. You see nothing happening. It feels like the battle is still raging and you don't know what to do next. This is your opportunity to stand. Standing means you know God is good. Psalms 145:9 *"The LORD is good to all, and His tender mercies are over all His works."* Standing means you remember Romans 8:28 *"And we know that all things work together for good to those who love God, to those who are the called according to His purpose."* Standing means you are not allowing fear to control you. Standing means you know you are not alone, but God is with you and your fellow believers are supporting you. Standing means you believe God gave you victory. 2 Corinthians 2:14 *"Now thanks be to God who* *always leads us in triumph in Christ, and through us diffuses the fragrance of His knowledge in every place."* Remember that your battle is in the spiritual realm. You are fighting principalities and powers and spiritual darkness. You can't see into the spiritual realm, so you may not immediately see the results of your warfare. When a warrior stands, he is protecting his position and his fellow soldiers while maintaining his victory over his enemy. Keeping your spiritual stance maintains your victory and defeats the enemy of God. You will see the results of your efforts, so do not lose heart. Stand strong.

- **Prayer and Supplication**. Prayer is communication with God. Prayer includes worship, thanksgiving, praise, repentance, and intercession. Prayer opens your heart and spiritual awareness to God's presence. Through prayer, you can not only offer worship to God, but you hear God as well. Prayer is a powerful weapon. It is time to connect with your Commander-in-Chief for battle strategies. In prayer, God will encourage, guide, teach and correct you in your daily walk. Praying opens the gate to God's power in your life and involves God in your fight. Therefore, the enemy does not want you to pray and will do everything he can to stop you from praying. Supplication is a prayer that directly petitions God for specific things. You may find yourself in circumstances that you don't know how to handle. Though the Bible has an answer for all things, you may not have the understanding regarding how to apply the Scriptures to your circumstance. You may have a specific need that requires a solution, and you can't see a way to meet the need. Supplication is bringing this need to God, humbling yourself to His will, and asking for help. The enemy wants to keep you sick and tired, lacking and wanting, discouraged and defeated. He knows that when you ask God for help, your Father hears, and will get involved in the situations. The enemy is afraid of the power of your prayers. Prayer is a way for you to pursue the enemy, so be persistent. (For a more in-depth look at prayer, please see book eight in the *Walking with Jesus* series "Time in the Garden.")

Continuing the Conquest

I saw a quote that said, "You were given this life because you are strong enough to live it." I don't know who wrote it, but I like it. 1 Corinthians 10:13 says, *"No temptation has overtaken you except such as is common to man; but God is faithful, who will not allow you to be tempted beyond what you are able, but with the temptation will also make the way of escape, that you may be able to bear it."* Whatever comes your way, even though it may feel unique and lonely, the situation is not unique. You are not the first one to have ever endured whatever it is and you won't be the last. The Lord prepared you with everything you need, and God is in the midst of the whole thing providing an escape and the strength to make it through. It's easy to forget that the attacks, struggles, and temptations are not really about you. You might like to think the attacks are directed specifically at us, but they aren't. The conflict is all about the clash between an all-powerful God and a raging rebellion. For a short time, the Lord is allowing Satan some room. This is not so Satan causes harm to individuals, but it is so you as a child of God have an opportunity to exercise your power over the enemy and learn your authority in the Kingdom. It isn't your battle, it's God's battle. 2 Chronicles 20:15b states, *"Thus says the* L*ORD* *to you: 'Do not be afraid nor dismayed because of this great multitude, for the battle is not yours, but God's."*

Part of your purpose on earth is to execute the authority of God over these enemy forces. Man is not the most powerful being in the universe, as some would like to believe. Satan, as an angelic being, was created with certain aspects that far exceed man's abilities. However, God chose you to be part of His army to defeat this rebellious order. This infuriates the enemy and makes me want to laugh at how amazing it is that God wants to use humankind to put Satan and his demonic followers in their place. It must be very humiliating to the enemy, and I love it. So, you need God's direction and guidance. It is through His power that you overcome. He fights for you and brings you victory. Exodus 14:13-14 *"Fear ye not, stand still, and see the salvation of the Lord, which he will shew to you today… The Lord shall fight for you, and ye shall hold your peace"* KJV. It's the Lord's battle. Not yours. He will lead you to triumph. 2 Corinthians 2:14, *"Now thanks be to God who always leads us in triumph in Christ, and through us diffuses the fragrance of His knowledge in every place."*

God reminds you repeatedly in the scriptures to utterly destroy the enemy. Don't just wound him and move on, but completely destroy whatever evil work the enemy is trying to do in your life. It's impossible to live at peace with the enemy. He will try to coexist with you, but don't do it. Coexisting with the enemy puts you in a serious threat of compromise. In the Old Testament, the Israelites were told by God to utterly destroy their enemies whenever challenged by enemy forces. However, they made a few treaties and spared some enemy forces allowing them to live among them and coexist. This proved very detrimental in the long run when the enemy influenced their life and distracted them from God and His purpose. The Israelites ended up in slavery. Don't play with the enemy of your soul. **UTTERLY DESTROY HIM**. Joshua provides an example in Joshua 8:26-27 *"For Joshua did not draw back his hand, with which he* *stretched out the spear, until he had utterly destroyed all the inhabitants of Ai. Only the livestock and the spoil of that city Israel took as booty for themselves, according to the word of the Lord which He had commanded Joshua".* Joshua left no survivors, and he walked away with the spoils. God expects you to do the same. You are to utterly destroy the enemy that assaults your life. Make no treaties and don't allow coexistence. This will prevent the enemy from wreaking havoc in your life from a covert position and protect you and yours from internal corruption.

Fear will try to dissuade you from the fight. Don't be afraid. Don't give up. You are equipped and ready. You are not alone and you are chosen. You are in His purpose and your victory is just around the corner. Keep trying and never give up. When you choose a godly, obedient lifestyle and do not waiver from your purpose, prosperity seeks you. Joshua 1:7 *"Only be you strong and very courageous, that you may observe to do according to all the law, which Moses my servant commanded you: turn not from it to the right hand or to the left, that you may prosper wherever you go"* AKJV. Be strong and very courageous so you can declare as Paul did to Timothy in 2 Timothy 4:7, *"I have fought the good fight, I have finished the race, I have kept the faith."*

God has given you the tools to be successful in your battles. You are fully equipped. The Lord already won the war. You are destined to succeed when you are in His will. The enemy doesn't have any new tricks. His battle plan is old. Strategies to stand against all of his tactics are in the Word of God. You have armor, weapons, strategies, the Word of God, and the Holy Spirit. That's everything you need to win.

Stepping Stones

1. Spiritual warfare is ongoing spiritual combat between God and satan.

2. The enemy will attempt to attack your body to inhibit the will of God.

3. The enemy will attempt to attack your soul to create doubt and unbelief.

4. The enemy will attempt to attack your spirit to destroy your relationship with the Lord.

5. The most common battlefield is your mind.

6. Attitude of a spiritual warrior includes an attitude of prayer, balance, reality, focus, dominion, obedience, and victory.

7. Your arsenal includes the blood of Jesus, the name of Jesus, prayer and fasting, obedience and submission, and praise and thanksgiving.

8. Wear the armor of God daily.

9. Jesus already won the war; your victory is secure.

10. Never give up.

I Am Strong

WALKING AS A WARRIOR

1. Identify three attitudes of a spiritual warrior. How can these be applied to your life?

2. Name five spiritual weapons. How do you plan to use your spiritual weapons?

3. Name three pieces of spiritual armor. What would change in your life if you wore spiritual armor?

4. Fill in the blanks of Ephesians 6:10-11.

   Finally my _____ be _____ in the _____ and in the _____ of His _____. _____ on the whole _____ of _____ that you may be _____ to _____ against the _____ of the _____.

5. What tactics does the enemy use against you?

Glossary

SIMPLE GLOSSARY OF A FEW WORDS FROM THE CHRISTIAN FAITH

Adultery - The act of being sexually unfaithful to one's spouse

Agape - Affection, goodwill, love, brotherly love, a love feast

Angel - Messenger of God

Apostasy - Turning away from the religion, faith, or principles that one used to believe

Apostle - One sent forth, one chosen and sent with a special commission as a fully authorized representative of the sender.

Atonement - To cover, blot out, forgive; restore harmony between two individuals.

Attribute – An inherent characteristic

Backslide - To go back to ungodly ways of believing or acting.

Blasphemy - Words or actions showing a lack of respect for God or anything sacred.

Bless - To make or call holy, to ask God's favor, to praise; to make happy.

Blessing - A prayer asking God's favor for something, something that brings joy or comfort.

Born-again – To be begotten or birthed from God, the beginning, to start anew

Carnal - Of the flesh or body, not of the spirit, worldly; seat of one's desires opposed to the spirit of Christ

Cherubim - Guardian angels, angels that guard or protect places

Commitment - A promise, a pledge

Conditional - Placing restrictions, conditions, or provisions to receive

Conversion - Turn, return, turn back; change

Convert - To change from one form or use to another, to change from one belief or religion to another.

Courtship - The act or process of seeking the affection of one with the intent of seeking to win a pledge of marriage

Covenant - A pledge, alliance, agreement

Cult - A body of believers whose doctrine denies the deity of Christ.

Deliverance - A freeing or being freed, rescue; the act of change or transformation.

Demon - Evil spirit

Devil - Principal title for satan, the archenemy of God and man

Dispensation - A period of time, sometimes called ages

Dominion - To rule over, have power over, overcome, exercise lordship over

Eros - Erotic, physical love

Eternal - Existing always, forever, without time

Evangelist - Proclaims the gospel of Jesus Christ

Faith - Believing, trusting, depending, and relying on God

Fellowship - Sharing, communion, partnership, intimacy

Forgiveness - To pardon, release from bondage

Fornication - To act like a harlot, to be unfaithful to God, illicit sexual intercourse

Glorification - Salvation of the body, transforming mortal bodies to eternal bodies

Grace - Unmerited favor of God, help given in the time of need from a loving God

Holy - Set apart, sacred

Intercession - To meet or encounter, to strike upon, to pray for another

Justification - Salvation of the spirit, just as if I never sinned

Marriage - A divine institution designed by God as an intimate union, which is physical, emotional, intellectual, social, and most importantly, spiritual

New Testament - Text of the new covenant

Offering - Everything you give beyond your tithe

Old Testament - Text of the old covenant

Omnipotent - All-encompassing power of God

Omnipresent - Unlimited nature of God, ability to be everywhere at all times

Omniscient - God's power to know all things

Pastor - Shepherds of the body of believers

Philia - Conditional love, based on feelings, friendships

Praise - Thanksgiving, to say good things about, words that show approval.

Prayer - Communication with God

Prophet - One who is a spokesperson for God, one who has seen the message of God and declares that message

Propitiation - To satisfy the anger of God, to gain favor; appease

Rapture - To be carried away, or the catching away of

Reconciliation - Restore harmony or fellowship between individuals, to make friendly again

Redemption - To buy back, to purchase, recover, to Rescue from sin

Regeneration - To give new life or force to, renew, to be restored, to make better, improve or reform, to grow back anew

Repent - To give new life or force, to renew, to be restored, to make better, improve or reform, to grow back a new.

Resurrection - A return to life subsequent to death

Revelation - The act of revealing or making known

Righteousness - Right standing with God, integrity, virtue, purity of life, correctness of thinking

Sacrifice - The act of offering something, giving one thing for the sake of another; a loss of profit

Salvation - Deliverance from any kind of evil whether material or spiritual, being saved from danger or evil; to rescue.

Sanctification - Salvation of the soul. Separation from the seduction of sin

Satan - The chief of fallen spirits, opponent; adversary

Sealing - Something that guarantees, a sign or token, to make with a seal to make it official or genuine

Sin - All unrighteousness, missing the mark, wrong or fault; violation of the law

Spirit - A being that is not of this world, has no flesh or bones

Steward - A guardian or overseer of someone else's property, manager

Supernatural - Departing from what is usual, normal, or natural to give the appearance of transcending the laws of nature

Talent - A natural skill that is unusual.

Tithe - Ten percent of all your increase

Tribulation - Distress, trouble, a pressing together, pressure, affliction

Trinity - Three in one: Father, Son, Holy Spirit

Unconditional - No restrictions, conditions, boundaries, demands, or specific provisions

Will – Choice, inclination, desire, pleasure, command, what one wishes or determines shall be done

About the Author

Pamela is a teacher, mentor, and author of the inspirational book *Destiny Arise* and children's books including *Time in a Tuna*. Pam earned her bachelor's degree at the University of Illinois Springfield, her master's degree in Organizational Leadership at Lincoln Christian University, and her doctorate in Leadership at Christian Leadership University. She serves as a mentor for the Spirit Life Circles sponsored by CLU.

She works from her home in the prairie land of central Illinois. Pam and her bodybuilding husband own a gym/fitness center that promotes living a balanced life. She taught sixth grade for almost twenty years. Pam also taught preschool through adult-age students in various venues. She served as director of Super Church, the children's ministry in the United Methodist Church in her hometown. Pam also served in the church nursery, as director of New Life Ministries Discipleship Program, Vacation Bible School Director, Kingdom Kids Children's Ministry Director, and Sunday School teacher. She has also been on missionary trips. Her favorite trip, so far, was the time she spent in Belize.

Pam enjoys kayaking, bicycling, and riding her motor scooter. When she isn't writing, she enjoys spending time with her four children and their families which includes five grandchildren who are the inspiration of her children's books.

Walking with Jesus Series

Becoming the Best Me I Can Be

Book 1 - There Must Be a Better Way

Walking in Salvation

Book 2 - Lord, I Need Help!

Walking with the Holy Spirit

Book 3 - I Thought I Was Changed

Walking in Transformation

Book 4 - I Am Supernatural

Walking in Spiritual Gifts

Book 5 - I Am Strong

Walking as a Warrior

Book 6 - I Am Fruitful

Walking in the Fruit of the Spirit

Book 7 - Love Letters from God

Walking in the Word

Book 8 - Time in the Garden

Walking in the Power of Prayer

Book 9 - I'm in Charge of What?

Walking in Stewardship

Book 10 - The End of – Well, Pretty Much Everything

Walking into Eternity

Who am I? What am I doing here? Where am I going? Everyone at some point in life asks these questions. You were wired to ask and engineered to pursue the answers. The road to discovering destiny is besieged by fiascoes, failures, and the agony of defeat. If your strength has been depleted and has caused you to give up, sit down, push pause, and snooze until another day, then this book is just for you! Amazing experiences are waiting for you. Get ready to be awakened from the posture of defeat, depression, and despair.

Destiny Arise is an easy-to-read book, providing tools to aid in living an amazing life. This book is designed as a trip adviser for your expedition. It will teach you how to evict the spirit of mediocrity and use your past to propel you into your future. You will learn how to shake off the common, arising to be an uncommon force taking your rightful place in the earth. You can change the world. I pray this book will ignite a passionate fire to pursue your destiny unapologetically. Destiny, awake from your slumber and arise.

www.ingramcontent.com/pod-product-compliance
Lightning Source LLC
Chambersburg PA
CBHW062158100526
44589CB00014B/1871